HOUNDS FOR A PACK

Also by Lionel R. Woolner

THE HUNTING OF THE HARE

an Anthology with Commentary

HOUNDS FOR A PACK

COMTE Élie de VEZINS

Translated and with an Introduction by
LIONEL R. WOOLNER

Foreword by
Sir Rupert Buchanan-Jardine

J. A. ALLEN

ISBN 85131 210 1

First published in France in 1882
at Montauban under the title
*Les Chiens Courants Francais pour
la Chasse du Lièvre dans le Midi de
la France*

© Lionel R. Woolner   1974
in respect of Introduction and
Translation

This first English translation published in 1974 by
J. A. Allen & Company Limited,
1 Lower Grosvenor Place,
Buckingham Palace Road,
London SW1W oEL

Set in 10/12 Linotype Pilgrim
and printed and bound by
John Sherratt and Son Limited
Altrincham, Cheshire

Contents

List of Illustrations

The first five of the above illustrations, drawn by Baron Karl Reille, first appeared in *'Parlons Venerie'*, edited and published in 1950 by Ferdinand Riant of 25, rue de Berri, Paris 8.

The above illustrations, painted by Baron Karl Reille, first appeared in *'Hounds of the World'* by Sir John Buchanan-Jardine, published by Methuen & Company in 1937.

Foreword

by

Sir Rupert Buchanan-Jardine, Bt., M.C., M.F.H.

In France the science of venery has always played a larger part in hunting than it has in this country, where the riding angle has been uppermost for a long time. I am sure that both hare-hunters and fox-hunters will find a great deal of interest in this work by the Comte de Vezins, which has been so ably translated by Mr. Woolner.

Some of the Comte de Vezins' views may appear rather unorthodox but certainly provide food for thought.

I agree entirely with his view that a small pack produces better sport than a large one: I used to have some of my best hunts with seven or eight couple. He also makes the point that working qualities such as nose and tongue are of more importance than conformation. I feel that this point is sometimes overlooked in this country where undue emphasis is placed on conformation.

I am sure that the Comte de Vezins would have agreed with William Somervile, the famous poet, in his approach to Hare Hunting. In his poem, 'The Chace', he writes:

A different hound for every different chace
Select with judgment; nor the timorous hare
O'er-matched destroy, but leave that vile offence
To the mean murd'rous coursing crew; intent
On blood and spoil. Oh blast their hopes, just Heaven.

And all their painful drudgeries repay
With disappointment and severe remorse.
But husband thou thy pleasures and give scope
To all her subtle play: by Nature led
A thousand shifts she tries; to unravel these
The industrious beagle twists his waving tail,
Through all her labyrinths pursues and rings
Her doleful knell.

Castle Milk   RUPERT BUCHANAN-JARDINE

Introduction

I T is generally known that the English system of hunting
with a pack of hounds, many of our hunting terms and even,
for the most part, the ancestors of our hounds, originated in
France. However, down the centuries, the general approach
to hunting in this country, with its emphasis on fox-hunting,
has tended to attach less importance than in France to the
finer points of hound work and our hunting literature reflects
this approach.

There is a very considerable French literature dealing with
the art of hunting and many of these books are devoted, in
whole or part, to detailed studies of various aspects of the
hunt. In particular, the finer points of the hunting of such
rusés quarries as the hare and the roe have received close
attention. In this country, on the other hand, our quite
voluminous literature of hunting has, with a very few exceptions, concerned itself far more with hunting history and
personalities and less with hounds and hound-work.

Our main pre-occupation, so far as hounds are concerned,
seems to be an unnecessarily close attention to conformation
with much less regard being paid to nose and, certainly,
voice. No one would deny that conformation should be
basically sound but, equally, many a first-rate working hound,
for example the great Furrier, has been in no way handi-
capped by minor imperfections. It is not so with regard to
nose and voice: anything but perfection in either of these
qualities must inevitably lessen a hound's ability and value.

This little work, a translation of a book, rare even in

France, written by Comte Élie de Vezins and published at Montauban in 1882 under the title of *"Les Chiens Courants Francais pour la Chasse du Lièvre dans le Midi de la France"*, is of a particularly specialised nature. It comprises a very thoughtful and closely-reasoned analysis of the various working methods and other qualities of hounds and suggests the best way of combining the differing abilities of individual hounds so as to put together in the most effective way a pack for hunting the hare. I know of no work in the English language which has attempted anything of the kind.

Comte de Vezins is particularly interesting in his ideas on the building up of a team led by the *chien de tête* and backed-up by the various types of *chiens de centre*. Some people may consider that all the hounds in a pack should be capable of operating equally skilfully in every aspect of the hunt but this does not seem to be a realistic conception. Hounds, like humans, have their individual skills and styles and we should no more expect to find them all equally expert in every aspect of hunting than expect a team of footballers all to play equally well in any position.

One knows of packs which tend to "flash" and over-run at a check through lack of a close-hunting hard-core to hold the line whilst the more ambitious hounds cast themselves widely. And one has also seen the pack which ties on the line and will not press forward because it has not the services of what the Comte de Vezins calls a *chien de tête* and *chiens seconds* to activate it.

The author's preference for cross-bred hounds may surprise English readers. In this country purity of blood has always been considered of major importance and any suggestion of an out-cross has, with few exceptions, been coldly received. In France, on the other hand, controlled cross-breeding is accepted as a sensible and legitimate method of improving a strain of hound and the great majority of French hounds, whatever their quarry, are frankly described as *Anglo-Poitevins-Saintongeois*, *bâtards de Haut Poitou*, *harriers Somerset-Griffon-Vendéen* etc.

Comte de Vezins claimed only a limited field for his ideas in applying them solely to the hunting of the hare in the South of France as practised there with French hounds but I feel that they can, with equal value, be applied to hare-hunting in this country. They may even have some application to the formation of a pack of foxhounds although, as the author makes clear, hare-hunting and fox-hunting are two very different things.

Comte de Vezins' pack, the Équipage de Vezins, had been mastered by his family for generations, passing from father to son. It generally consisted of eight or ten couple of Gascon-Saintongeois hounds, blue-mottled or black and white, hunting only hare and killing from twelve to fifteen brace a season. From September until December the pack was hunted around Vezins, near Angers in northern France, but at the turn of the year, when driven south by the snow, the pack was moved to Montauban, near Toulouse, and hunted in the forest of Montech. Apart from its reputation as a hunting pack considerable success was achieved at hound shows. The Hunt continued in existence at least up to 1914 but then seems to have fallen victim to the first World War.

I have left in the original French the names of the various groups of hounds into which the author divides his ideal pack because, a measure perhaps of our lack of interest in this aspect of hound study, we have, except for the road-hound, no English equivalent. Certain other expressions have, for the same reason, been left in French but, where necessary, their meaning has been made clear by foot-notes.

I am greatly indebted to Sir Rupert Buchanan-Jardine for his Foreword. He and his late father, Sir John, have for many years bred and hunted the Dumfriesshire Foxhounds, a pack of black hounds with tan markings which, although based on the English Foxhound, has received a substantial admixture of bloodhound and Gascon-Saintongeois blood for the purpose of improving nose, voice and general hunting ability. The Count de Vezins would undoubtedly have approved of such breeding.

It is not, I think, generally known that Sir Rupert has also been a keen hare-hunter. Prior to the War he hunted hare in Scotland with a pack of the rough-coated Griffon Vendéen Bassets bred from imported French stock. Here, again, he found the pure-bred hound capable of improvement and that a beagle out-cross helped to steady the rather impetuous hunting style of the Griffon.

I should also like to acknowledge the assistance given me by M. Ashley Dormeuil in connection with both the translation of certain of the French hunting terms and research into the history of Comte de Vezins and his Équipage.

L.R.W.

Preface

H U N T I N G with a pack of hounds in the South of France survives now only as an exception. It is reduced, in general, to that of the hare which, by its many ruses and the very light scent which it leaves behind, makes its pursuit most difficult and its taking very problematical.

The hunting of the hare does not produce the brilliant *mis en scène* or the exciting spectacle provided by the hunting of the larger beasts of the chase but it fascinates true hunting men for it is one of the most scientific forms of hunting and, in spite of its modest *rôle*, is considered as the school and the key to the art of venery.

To *force* a hare, that is to say to take with a pack of hounds alone the most cunning of animals, of which the track is so light that it leaves scarcely any scent, one must possess an excellent pack of hounds and, to breed up such a pack, must understand fully the qualities and faults of the hound. Such is the study which we wish to make with care for it appears to us to comprise primary and indispensible ideas for every disciple of St. Hubert. We shall examine this subject in a very restricted field, applied only to French hounds bred in the South of France and intended for the style of hunting which is practised there. If we stray outside these limits our reflections would be little understood and would have lost their real application.

The craze for killing quickly has frequently modified not only the type and quality of the hound but also the manner of hunting the hare. To hunt at the greatest possible pace is the end aimed at by many huntsmen : to "mop up" the quarry one way or another and account for it in 40 or 45 minutes on good scenting days is the result desired by some but which we have never been able to appreciate. In our view all the merit, all the interest of hare-hunting lies in the contest between the skill and cunning of the quarry and the intelligent work of a good pack. We cannot accept that one may sacrifice the cry or the skill of the pack for sheer speed and that, as a result of the urge to kill as quickly as possible, a headlong pursuit, constantly backed up by the ready interference of the huntsman, may be substituted for the fascinating work of a clever pack.

Most hunting men in the South agree with this approach and, whilst trying to press on with the hunt, have preserved the special character of hare-hunting. Our huntsmen have understood that, in order to *force* an animal which keeps going for scarcely two hours before a steady and sustained hunt, excessive speed is not necessary; and that, in our very cultivated country, the hound should be clever enough to work without assistance at checks and that it is necessary, above all, to establish the skill of the pack before uniting to it that of the huntsman.

PART ONE

The ABC of the Subject

THE TYPE OF HOUND

Several types of hound are used for hare-hunting in the South of France: they present many variations, according to their origins, but can be placed in the following three categories:

1. The pure-blooded *grand chien* or *chien d'ordre*, whether of Gascony, Saintonge or Bordeaux.
2. *The Briquet.**
3. The cross-bred hound or the improved *briquet*.

The *Chien d'ordre*, or pure hound, which only a few enthusiasts have, with great trouble, preserved in all its original purity, has some fine qualities: great acuteness of nose, a direct, brilliant and active style of hunting and a magnificent voice. He is clever, sensible, easy to discipline and has a great deal of stamina but, for hare-hunting he is slack, slow in his work and does not work persistently at checks. He casts himself listlessly and unintelligently, becomes clever only at the end of his career and always needs the help of the huntsman. His great size makes him suitable only for the flat country, he gets out of breath on the hills, runs unhappily over stony ground where his feet get cut and

* Note: The *briquet* is a harrier-sized hound, of much the same breeding as the various breeds of French hounds but often cross-bred and sometimes not even entirely of hound blood.

heat up and he needs a great deal of attention in kennel because his health is generally delicate.

We prefer, then, for the delicate hunting of the hare a type of hound which is a better worker and more intelligent, leaving to the *chien d'ordre* the chase of the larger animals to which it is more suited.

The *briquet* is a very active and intelligent hound and sometimes produces really remarkable individuals. He is very suitable for hunting, a couple or two at a time, in conjunction with the gun, when he makes up for lack of numbers by his activity and skill but one cannot turn *briquets* into an organised pack for ordinary hunting. They are, in general, either violent and unmanageable or too *collés** and *nazillards***. They are not correct or direct in their work, have poor voices, pack badly, do not like cold scents and are most undisciplined.

The *chien d'ordre* and the *briquet* being ruled out we are left with the cross-bred hound which, on the whole, we prefer and which seems to us the most suitable, in our country, for hare-hunting. We shall upset some people by this choice but as our opinion is purely a personal one and we do not seek to impose it on others we have no hesitation in expressing it.

The cross-bred hound, bred from a cross between a pure-bred hound and a *briquet*, unites the virtues of both types and often gets rid of the defects. He gets from the pure hound a better nose and more stamina than the *briquet*, more steadiness and sagacity in his style of working, a better voice, more discipline and a better conformation. From the *briquet* he inherits more intelligence and ability together

---

* Note : A hound is described as *collé* (literally "stuck") when he ties on the line and does not get forward.

** *Nazillard* (literally "snuffler") implies the same thing.

Black and tan hounds

Griffons

with better health than the pure hound, more activity in his work and greater persistence at checks.

Our hound, then, for hare-hunting as we conduct it, is the cross-bred hound or the improved *briquet*, standing 19" or 20", with a good voice, lightly-built and cleanly-coloured, able to hunt as well in the hills as in the plain.

THE PACK

The creation of a pack with which to hunt the hare requires a wise plan and a judicious choice of the individuals selected to compose it. A good pack should comprise several kinds of working qualities which, intelligently combined, will contribute to final success and the taking of the hare.

The hounds, by their individual and different contributions, should help each other, working together to hold the line and all following it as quickly as possible. They should not, then, all have the same qualities for in that case they would do the same work and three or four such hounds would be just as effective as a larger pack of them. The whole advantage of a pack is that it can combine many special qualities, each having their undoubted uses.

If one hunts only with the gun a few steady hounds will suffice to drive the unfortunate hare to you sooner or later. But if one undertakes the development and expense of a proper pack, if one wishes to attain the pleasure of hunting solely with hounds, one must start with this principle: that to account for hares it is necessary to push on surely and quickly and that one will only attain this result with hounds having different working qualities. One must group at the centre a solid core of hounds who can maintain the line with certainty and activate this group with other, enterprising hounds. In a word, one must combine sagacity and steadiness with drive and decision, that is the end to attain. The differing styles do not hinder the joint action: hounds

B

of differing styles, hunting at the same speed and having a complete understanding between them will always hunt together.

A large pack is not necessary to account for a hare. The task of getting a good pack together is arduous enough without adding to the difficulties by a useless and often dangerous expansion. Furthermore, a great number of hounds will frighten the small landowners of the South who allow us, somewhat unwillingly, to hunt their broken-up lands and who are ready at the least pretext to withdraw permission. A dozen well-chosen working hounds are sufficient to unravel all ruses and overcome all difficulties. They will suffice also for music, that orchestra so agreeable to the huntsman's ear, and to secure, in the South of France, all the self-esteem of their Master. But one must be without pity for all hounds which do not apply themselves seriously to their work, and sell, give away or put down all individuals which do nothing to help. It is better to have only a few good hounds rather than a larger number, some of which hinder the work of the others. We do not refer here to young hounds, a harsh necessity which one has to put up with in the interests of the future of the pack.

The pack, above all, must be of the same *pied*, that is to say, the hounds which compose it should hunt at the same pace: no brilliant fellows forging ahead, no stragglers, but a combined and compact group acting together. The hound who is putting all his effort into keeping up with his fellows gets out of breath and is in no state to do any useful work or to render any service. The hounds of a pack, then, should hunt without effort, without hindrance and without fatigue.

The pace, in our view, should be neither slow nor excessively fast. If too slow it increases all the difficulties, permitting the hare to get too far ahead and to play tricks of greater complexity, so doubling its chances of escape. If too rapid it becomes subject to a host of inconveniences which we will indicate and develop later. A vigorous and sustained pace, permitting the taking of a large hare in two hours is assuredly what we prefer.

The breed, number and pace once decided on we shall put together our pack in the following way, enlarging on each of the various types, which we specify as follows:

Chien de tête;

Chiens de centre: which we sub-divide into *chiens de centre pur, chiens de centre avancé* and *chiens seconds;*

Chiens de chemin

CHIEN DE TETE

The expression *chien de tête* is sometimes used to refer to every hound of great ability who, by his experience and working qualities, distinguishes himself in a pack by a real superiority. In our region of the South this term has quite a different meaning: it does not refer to the general ability of a hound but solely to his style of hunting.

We call *chien de tête* the hound which, endowed with great resolution and bold in his work, has the ability to follow the scent easily and swiftly and who, helped also by a slightly superior speed, places himself at the head of the pack to lead it swiftly on the track of the quarry.

The skills of the *chien de tête* are quite special: they permit him to carry the hunt forward without hesitation and to give it real impulsion and drive.

He is so named, then, not only because of his speed but also because his style of hunting distinguishes him from others in that he tries always to drive on and has the instinct to cast himself widely and forward at the head of the pack.

This different type of leader is not accepted by all Masters of

Hounds and opinions on this subject are often contradictory. Some believe that hounds should take the lead indiscriminately, not necessarily retaining it, and position themselves from time to time according to the various phrases of the hunt. On the other hand others affirm the usefulness of one hound generally holding the first position and habitually leading the pack. We share the latter opinion, relying on the following considerations which we submit to the observation and experience of hare-hunters.

The packs which come closest to perfection are, as we have said, those which are sagacious, steady and at the same time very active, and we believe that the *chien de tête* contributes to the combination of these qualities.

The *chien de tête*, easily dominating his comrades, not only by his greater speed but by his particular ability to follow the scent boldly, prevents any dispute which might be fatal to the balance of the pack. He imposes his wisdom on ambitious hounds which, because they are obliged to submit to his leadership, lose any tendency to wildness and haste. He forces each to remain in his place and to position himself correctly within the pack. The hounds thus controlled and held on the line, do not dare either to lose it or to hold the pack back and, like a flock of migrant birds, allow the most enterprising to place himself at their head and follow him with confidence and certainty.

In addition the *chien de tête* livens the pack and communicates to it by his drive and decision a forward impulse which, extending through the pack, permits neither hesitation nor indecision.

The hound which regularly leads in this way acquires, furthermore, a complete perfection in his *rôle*. He accomplishes his task with sagacity because he has no rivals; he holds the line well and keeps the leadership with a certainty of direction which often leads to success. A pack without such a leader may hunt well but never with the initiative, the speed of action and sustained drive which is communicated by the *chien de tête*.

We will pose this argument to those who think otherwise. If every hound is to take the lead indiscriminately a pack would have to be composed either of *chiens de centre* or of hounds having the character of *chiens de tête*. In the first case the pack would hunt correctly but slowly, without drive or decision : it would check often, not because of any fault but because the quarry would have time to take a good lead, to multiply its ruses and to leave, the further it drew away, a scent which, becoming slowly weaker, would in the end disappear completely. In the second case, the pack, composed of leaders who will have in turn the pleasure of an unfoiled and consequently very attractive line, will be driven on by a body of ambitious hounds who will struggle, panting, for the first place and hinder all correct hunting.

Having considered these reflections and warnings let us examine the qualities required of the *chien de tête*. His responsibilities are so great that one cannot go to too much trouble in selecting him and requiring from him a number of qualities indispensible to the importance of his *rôle*.

In the choice of a good *chien de tête* one must consider sagacity, scenting ability, drive, voice, stamina, speed and conformation.

Sagacity. The *chien de tête* should be sensible; that is to say his desire to lead should not encourage him to be first, come what may. Enterprising by nature he is always a little eager since one cannot find a leader entirely without ambition but one must select a hound who has not too much of it, who does his work calmly and whose rapid and decisive work is carried out without violence, without haste and never to the detriment of the line.

The sagacity of the *chien de tête*, then, consists in his not letting himself be carried away by his natural eagerness to enjoy the scent and, whilst driving on with decision, keeping enough control of himself to be able to stop when he can no longer own the line.

Scenting ability. For a *chien de tête* scenting ability is of more importance than for any other type of hound. It permits him to accomplish his work with certainty, never hesitating to follow the line boldly, nor involving the whole pack in a check by over-running the line.

The hounds which compose the body of the pack back up and support each other but the *chien de tête*, alone in front and dependent only on himself, cannot rely on the skill of his fellows and depends on his own ability and the acuteness of his nose for the accuracy of his course. The low-scenting hound is, moreover, brilliant in his work: he neither ties on the line nor hunts heel and can follow with his nose high.

Drive. Drive derives from sagacity combined with great scenting ability. Every sagacious hound with a good nose hunts without hesitation. If he hesitates, if he "comes and goes", it is because his nose is not good enough, as a result of which he has to work more actively, or because he has not enough patience and calmness to keep the line. He "flaps" about the place, runs up and down on the line and hunts only in fits and starts. The *chien de tête* on the other hand, who has a good nose and great sagacity, follows effortlessly the line run by the hare and maintains it, head high.

Voice. The importance of voice cannot be over-stressed in the choice of a leader. It should be strong and resounding so that it rallies the pack promptly and can be easily heard by the whole body of hounds. If the *chien de tête* has a poor voice he cannot easily rally the pack when a check is relieved as a result of his work in front and, since his style of hunting and his speed encourage him to press on with the scent, he would soon out-distance the main body who, not having heard him immediately, would often have trouble in catching up.

Stamina and Speed. The work of the chien de tête is the hardest and most tiring and has to be carried out whilst holding first place. Stamina and slightly superior speed are, then, absolutely necessary to ensure his *rôle* as leader and without these qualities he cannot sustain a quick and unhesitating style of hunting. If unable to keep easily in the lead he will wear himself out by his efforts and will finish by slowing down and letting the others pass him. His qualities and his services will then be useless at the moment when the difficulties become more numerous and one has most need of the skill and assistance of the whole pack. The *chien de tête* should lead without difficulty but without trying to out-distance his fellows: he should run a speed which will keep him in front but will not force the others to adopt a pace which they cannot maintain.

The leader who is not certain that he can dominate his fellows becomes over-eager, presses on and is often at fault for fear of seeing his place taken over, a place which every hound desires to maintain when he has occupied it for a long time. Also one cannot tolerate two *chiens de tête* in the same pack; they will think of nothing but competing with each other for first place; they will force the pace, hinder the regularity of the hunt and gradually disorganise the best pack.

Stylish hunting and Conformation. Beauty of form and

stylish hunting are not indispensible qualities but we would say to those who do not agree that if any hound ought to have these advantages it is assuredly the *chien de tête* for, running in the lead, he takes the eye and attracts observation more than any other. His work being more advanced is always noticeable and ought to give him the reputation of a "brilliant leader", praise which relates to the combination of all his qualities.

The *chien de tête* adding to the various qualities which we have just discussed experience and skill, we think that we have dealt sufficiently with this type of hound which we regard as so useful for the hunting of the hare.

THE CHIENS DE CENTRE

The *chiens de centre* constitute the main body of the pack and, according to their varying styles of hunting, can be placed in three classes as follows:

Chiens de centre pur, chiens de centre avancé and *chiens seconds.*

Chiens de Centre Pur. The *chiens de centre pur* constitute the hard-core of every well-organised pack. They form a group which, tied to the line, maintains it with certainty and patience. Without ambition, they do not seek to gain ground but to indicate and hold the line taken by the hare, leaving to the more enterprising hounds the task of carrying it forward. They follow these hounds without allowing themselves to be deflected from the line, to which they recall those hounds which diverge from it or over-run.

One should never hesitate to reinforce this hard-core of *chiens de centre pur* because they never compete with each other but give mutual assistance with a perfect understanding. They are usually superior in dealing with doubles and on bad scenting days their persistence and application unravel the line on difficult ground when other hounds become frustrated or tired with so many difficulties.

The *chien de centre pur* has sometimes the fault of being obstinate, cautious and a little inclined to hang on the line. This fault should be corrected and shows the necessity for other hounds with more drive and for a good *chien de tête*.

The good *chien de centre pur* should follow his fellows readily, not yard by yard, and should press forward without difficulty or delay.

Chiens de centre avancé. The *chien de centre advancé*, whilst having all the distinguishing characteristics of his type, is more enterprising, more decided, than the *chien de centre pur.* He pushes on more boldly, is more active in his work and at a check detaches himself better, makes his cast more rapidly and, in fact, acts more readily and promptly.

It is impossible to find in a hound more qualities combined than in a *chien de centre avancé.* In a very small pack he can at a pinch take the place of both the *chien de tête* and the *chien de centre pur* because of his balanced and forceful style of working. We would advise those who, by reason of their circumstances, the country where they live, or any other reason, are limited to a very few hounds, to choose a few *chiens de centre advancé* and to hunt with them. But to those who wish to organise a proper pack we say again that all the various types of hounds represent between them all the skills and, in consequence, every means of success.

Chiens Seconds. The *chiens seconds* are to be found amongst the most determined of the *chiens de centre avancé*. Their work, without having all the initiative and all the development of the *chien de tête*, is not dissimilar and presents certain analogies. Very active on the scent they have not as prompt and driving a style, do not seek to vie with the leader and are content with second place.

The *chiens seconds* have a really useful *rôle* in the pack: they contribute to its activity, are a link between the leader and the *chiens de centre* and have also the great advantage of making the *chien de tête* watchful, of preventing any slackness in his work and of replacing him momentarily if he weakens or makes a mistake. We do not, however, advise any exaggeration in the use of *chiens seconds*. Two or three are quite sufficient in any pack and they could introduce too much liveliness if there are too many of them.

CHIENS DE CHEMIN

The *chien de chemin* is so named because he has the precious quality of detecting the scent of the hare on the tracks and roads. This speciality is inborn and apparent as soon as he starts hunting.

One might think, at first, that a hound so endowed has a better nose than the others and that he can scent better on difficult ground. This view is not quite correct: one sees remarkable *chiens de chemin* which whilst questing and hunting-on carry the line no better than their fellows. This quality is, then, an exceptional skill which is improved and perfected by age and experience.

The *chien de chemin* understands perfectly that he is endowed with this advantage and applies himself to discovering on roads and on hard, stony ground the scent left by the hare. There, where his fellows recognise their powerlessness and perhaps even cease to work, the *chien de chemin* works persistently and finishes by establishing the line which one had believed lost, having thus the honour and the merit of overcoming one of the most difficult of ruses, a ruse which a hare multiplies as the hunt proceeds, its instinct indicating it as the best.

The chien de chemin is, then, indispensible in a pack. He is so precious that it is always very difficult to come across good hounds of this type. *The chiens de chemin* can belong either to the class of *chiens de tête* or that of *chiens de centre*: his particular skill does not imply any particular type but we prefer him to be a *chien de centre* for the following reason.

The great majority of hounds, as we have said, are unable to follow the scent well on roads and paths and it is at this moment that the *chien de chemin* deploys all his resources and takes the lead. If the *chien de chemin* belongs to the category of *chiens de tête* he will follow swiftly as soon as he has hit-off on this hard ground the scent which the others cannot own. The pack, undecided and hesitating to rally to him, will lose time and leave themselves even further behind as the *chien de tête*, having the double advantage of being the *chien de chemin* and of being able to carry the scent on rapidly, takes a lead which can be reduced only with difficulty and fatigue.

If, on the other hand, the *chien de chemin* is a *chien de centre* he will hold the line without hurrying himself and will give his comrades time to get to him and put themselves on the line without straggling.

The *chien de chemin* should inspire complete confidence and therefore must not be a babbler nor speak falsely. A babbler upsets the whole pack but they quickly discover that he deceives them and do not listen to the liar. On a road, however, they cannot themselves own anything and if the *chien de chemin* speaks falsely they follow him, letting themselves be led into an error which they could not foresee. We advise the acquisition of two *chiens de chemin* so that one may confirm the other and there can never be a false indication. Then the pack, which may hesitate when one hound alone speaks on the line, will follow quite confidently when two speak simultaneously.

Old hounds whom age and experience have rendered wise and cunning sometimes become *chiens de chemin* at the end of their career but unhappily their services are of short duration.

The *chien de chemin* should also combine the qualities of the type to which he belongs. Endowed, then, with all these advantages he is of great value, since out of a great many hounds one finds scarcely one good *chien de chemin*.

There are also to be found amongst hounds some with a particular style of hunting which we have deliberately omitted in the composition of the pack. We refer to the hound which runs around trying to cut off corners. His distinguishing characteristic is that he does not wish to tie himself to the line and work with the body of the pack. He places himself to a flank busying himself only with marking the twists of the hare and her changes of direction. He does his work on the flank as the *chien de tête* does his at the head of the column. This type of hound, liked by some but absolutely condemned by others, seems to us to be generally dangerous and we admit that it can only be tolerated in certain conditions.

One distinguishes two types of this skirting hound: those which hunt in this way from the beginning of their career, and ambitious *chiens de tête* which can no longer lead. The latter should be got rid of without delay. Being unable to reconcile themselves to remaining in the middle of the pack they try to cut corners so as to snatch for a moment the lead and take an advance which enables them to hold their place for as long as possible. Also they are very independent in their work and too eager when the line is hit-off. In consequence they bring to the pack only disorder and fatigue.

The skirter who hunts in this style from the beginning

is more sagacious and much less lively and ambitious. He can be tolerated when he works close to the pack, works calmly at the checks without pressing and has a good voice so that he can be clearly heard. When one usually hunts in open country, where there is not much risk of changing, the advantage of the skirter is that for most of the time he is a worker, clever, very good at refinding the hare and that his work on the flanks often avoids the troubles arising from doubles and thus advances the hunt. Nevertheless, we repeat that we consider that this *chien de coupé* is generally dangerous and we do not advise his inclusion in the pack.

PART TWO

The General Qualities of Hounds

Having dealt with special and necessary qualities of each
type of hound we will say something of the general merits
which should be found in every hound. The absence of
these, or the presence of contrary qualities, would result
in several faults which we will also indicate.

The general characteristics of hounds can be divided into
two categories: those which are linked with its instincts, its
intelligence and its work generally, and those which comprise all the advantages which spring from its conformation
and physical qualities. We shall call the first "mental
qualities" and the second "physical qualities".

I. MENTAL QUALITIES

In assessing the mental qualities of the hound one should
consider:

> Whether he is sagacious and steady.
> Whether he is really *requérant.**
> Whether he carries the line forward and is active.
> Whether he can be trusted.

Sagacity and Sensibility: The hound should be intelligent
and sensible; that is to say he should hunt calmly and
methodically with the sole object of contributing to the pack
his share of skill and work. He should make complete

---

* Note: *Réquerant*, as later explained, is the ability to cast and
work persistently at the checks: the ability to fresh-find the
hare or the line.

common cause with his fellows, listen to them and understand that he is there to help them and not simply to act alone and as his fancy dictates. He should be regular in his work, that is he should follow and keep the scent which he has found and not leave it in order to work further afield.

Every hound which is too eager and becomes over-excited is a menace to the pack. He carries the disorder with him, runs in every direction without attaching himself to the scent and tries only to hunt by himself so that he alone can succeed. Young hounds, spoiled by his example, become unsteady and irregular in their work; old hounds, disconcerted and upset, finish by dashing ahead or to the side. In a word it needs only one or two of these stupid hounds to disorganise the best pack.

One should not confuse the vice of the unsteady hound with the ignorant enthusiasm of the young hound just beginning to hunt. Youngsters cannot at once possess the experience and steadiness of their elders and are subject to faults arising solely from their youth. The young hound which is a real model of sagacity when it starts hunting very often does not turn out to be one of those brilliant hounds which rise above the ordinary level to become quite superior. All first-class hounds begin with more initiative, more keenness and more faults but when experience has calmed their first fire and has given them skill and knowledge they have crossed the barrier of ordinariness in front of which so many beginners remain.

The most sagacious and steady hounds are the *chiens d'ordre* or pure hounds but they sometimes exaggerate this quality, common to their breed, to such an extent that it becomes a fault.

Requérant : A hound can be considered really *requérant* when, the pack having for some reason or other lost the line, he seeks it again with intelligence, persistence and activity : when he works resolutely and with tenacity at the checks and does not allow himself to be discouraged either by their length or by the difficulties involved.

He examines first the areas immediately adjoining the point of check; then, if this work is in vain, he makes wider casts and finally detaches himself boldly, recognising that some unusual cause prevents him from recovering the line within this area and that he must try beyond the poor scenting ground which often hinders the most skilful casting.

The good *requérant*, then, casts himself widely, acting without hesitation and then, perhaps, at the moment when one begins to despair and all seems lost, one is thrilled by a well-loved voice announcing that the scent is refound. One's pleasure is then doubled by the overcoming of the difficulty.

We consider that this ability as a good *requérant* is the most essential, the most indispensible for every hound. It is, in our eyes, synonymous with skill, cleverness and working ability and we affirm that without it a hound cannot be outstanding and really superior. A hound may be clever, steady and have a fine nose but if he is not *requérant* he will be quite incomplete : his work will come to an end at the first difficulty and he will be unable to utilise his skills.

We admit that all hounds with some experience can disentangle those lesser ruses of the hare which cause what we call a *balancé* or hesitation but for the real check, for those inexplicable difficulties which discourage hounds and huntsman the good *requérant* alone can succeed in surmounting them and, rallying his ignorant and lazy fellows, will often become the hero of a brilliant kill.

Hounds which are bad *requérants* work for a short time in a small area, make a little cast, thinking that they have to deal only with a change of direction then, astonished and

Hounds working at a check

Hounds fresh-finding hare

not knowing how to deal with the situation they return to the point of check. They remain there undecided, waching the work of their fellows and if the check is prolonged they do no more work, waiting for the huntsman to come to their aid or following him about without troubling further about hunting.

How will a pack which does not *requête* well operate? One can have a very fine, energetic and clever huntsman but what will be his resources with disheartened hounds which are unwilling to assist any effort? Perhaps with the protection of St. Hubert the line will, in the end, be refound but with what trouble and what loss of time!

One can, if necessary, tolerate in a large pack a few hounds which are poor *requérants* if they have other merits, but in a small pack one should not hesitate: one must get rid of them without delay if one does not wish to suffer at the first check a probable loss and to see many hunts terminate in this sad way.

The method of the *requête* is not carried out in the same way by all good *requérants*: it varies in accordance with their general style of hunting. Determined hounds detach themselves at once and cast themselves widely and swiftly. The *chiens de centre* work in a smaller circle or operate at or near the point where they last had the line. This last method is not greatly appreciated by some huntsmen who allow themselves to be too dominated by their particular ideas. We do not share their views. Hounds which work at and around the point of check are very useful in a pack, in which there should be only a few of them. They complement the hounds which work more widely and make an important contribution to the operations of the pack, particularly on bad scenting days. In working step by step on the line they try to recover it where the others have left it to make their casts. Above all they are valuable when the

C

hare is sinking. At this moment when the quarry, having no more strength for flight, doubles on its tracks and squats frequently they almost always fresh-find her whilst the hounds which have detached themselves are liable to leave her inside the circle of their cast.

The *chien d'ordre* would be brilliant if he were a good *requérant* but unhappily he usually lacks this skill and cannot dispense with the assistance of the huntsman.

We will end this section by insisting as strongly as possible on the importance to be attached to this ability to be a good *requérant*. It is, as far as the hound is concerned, the principle from which spring the great superiorities.

Drive and Activity: When a hound has discovered the trace of the hare and has the scent he should work forward, that is to say, drive on without hesitation in the direction of the scent. If he loses it he should seek to refind it by a forward cast. He should have the instinct to extend his activities in a forward direction and should return to examine the flanks and rear only when his first efforts have proved fruitless.

One calls him "very active" when he does not tie on the line, follows it boldly and loses no time in hesitations and indecisions. Active hounds are diligent in their work, rally quickly, follow their comrades freely and are what Du Fouilloux called "hounds of heart and enterprise".

Every hound which does not get forward remains where he is or works back which, in different degrees, are serious faults. If he remains where he is he has no opportunity to recover the line: he waits endlessly, without decision at the point of check and one is obliged to get him moving and direct him. If he works back he not only does not assist but upsets things: he leads the pack back to places already examined, far from the point where they could hit off the line and thus complicates all the difficulties in a fatal manner. The hound which has the vice of working back should be got rid of immediately.

One can turn a blind eye to a hound which has other merits and tolerate it in a pack numerous enough to hide its faults but it would be unpardonable to tolerate it when it destroys the work of others. Hounds which work backwards undoubtedly destroy, by their pernicious action, the wise organisation of the best packs.

The inconvenience of the hound which has little activity is not as great as that of the hound which works back but in remaining a supporter of the *collé* hound we condemn too much of that quality : that is to say, the hound which is too *collé*.

The good hound should be steady and active at all times.

The hound which is too *collé* is without initiative and judgment. Accustomed only to tie himself to the line and to understand only the imprint of the hare, he takes an eternity to accomplish what the active hound does in a moment and as soon as he lacks the scent he is so astonished, so disturbed, that he can no longer act with judgment.

He can, however, have a use in the early part of the day, when questing up to the hare, and we condemn above all the excess of this factor only when the hare has been started. We will explain as briefly as possible what we have in mind.

When one has found the morning trail of the hare which, before dawn, retires to its form, the one object at that time is to discover the form and start the hare. The important thing then is to be led with certainty to this refuge; the slowness of the work and the loss of time do not matter since the hare will not move until dislodged. The very *collé* hound has its value at this time : it controls the ardour of its comrades, maintains absolutely the line, follows it step by step and advances with care and sagacity. But once the quarry is started things are entirely different. Frightened by the noise and sight of the pack the hare leaves rapidly and waits no longer in her form whilst one surmounts the difficulties which she may have left in her approach to it. She flies quickly across the fields, the roads and the places best suited to losing the scent: understanding all her danger she tries to put a great distance between herself and her enemies and draws on her best and finest ruses.

It is in the second half of the hunt, in the Second Act if we may so express it, that the inconvenience of the hound which is *collé* becomes serious and real. Now one must not only proceed with certainty but must act quickly and without loss of time. One aspires no longer to a stationary *dénouement* which by its immobility permits a careful and slow search, one pursues an end which flies on with rapidity. To account for a hare is a task serious enough, complicated enough, even doubtful enough without increasing the difficulties which lie in one's way.

Every hare which has the opportunity to get a good lead has many chances of saving herself because she can multiply all her means of defence. In the first place, the scent which she leaves as she passes will, as time elapses, become substantially weaker and on a bad scenting ground may evaporate completely. Then, little frightened by a slow and distant pursuit, she utilises all the resources of her imagination to multiply and complicate her ruses. She can easily execute them whilst speeding on and can adopt a calm and unhurried manner which permits her to defend herself for four or five hours, which will render her taking very problematical.

The slow and too *collé* hound has the serious inconvenience of never pressing the hare and bringing her nearer. His straggling and indecisive methods always hold him back. He loses precious time whilst hounds are running and more still at the checks. His lack of boldness holds him back, prolongs his work and permits the quarry to push forward and get always further away.

The pace of a hunt does not depend only on the speed at which hounds are capable of running; it depends to a great extent on their style of hunting. We do not, then, believe in the value of these too *collés* hounds if they have to rely upon themselves. The help of the huntsman and of more decided hounds can do no more than lessen their bad dispositions and faulty activities.

We end our reflections on this subject by citing the view of M. de la Conterie,* if we may be permitted to rely on the authority of his verdict.

> "Beware of the type of *clabauds*, hounds of little activity and so *collés* that they are an hour traversing one acre of the woods".

Babbling. To speak at the right time, certainly and truthfully, is a quality of real importance for a hound. By this means he notifies his fellows that he has found a trace or scent of the quarry and summons them to share his discovery. But if he gives false information, whether through eagerness, thoughtlessness, or real vice, he seriously disrupts the pack. He deceives them, worries them by his cry and calls them away from work which may be on the point of being successful to lead them in a false and opposite direction.

Not only does he disturb and discourage the pack but he irritates the huntsman himself, giving him a vain hope and a misleading indication which complicates the difficulties.

Babblers should not be confused with hounds of high nose. The first speak to anything without certainty or truth : the

---

* Note : Leverrier de la Conterie is well-known as the author of "L'Ecole de la Chasse aux Chiens Courants ou Venerie Normand", first published in 1763.

others also give tongue easily but it is because the fineness of their nose permits them to acknowledge the scent of the hare and to inhale the waves and light odours of the oldest scent. They speak, then, often alone because they have the superiority of scenting ability. Every Master of Hounds will quickly appreciate the difference to which we have drawn attention and, knowing his pack, will have no doubts in this respect.

The babbler is merely imperfect if he is mute at the checks, but if he speaks without cause at this most critical moment, if he lies or keeps speaking at the point of check, he cannot be kept in a good pack. His vice is in our view almost as great as that of the hound which works back on the line and in designating these two faults as the most dangerous we do not exaggerate because they stop, both of them, the work of the best packs.

The hound too short of voice who speaks little also has his inconveniences. He does not immediately notify his comrades nor rally them on the scent which he has found. Accordingly precious time is lost in not having the benefit of the skill and work of the rest of the pack. His muteness springs either from a lack of nose which prevents him from absorbing the particles of scent in a certain enough manner to enable him to announce it well and boldly, or from an egotistical vice which makes him keep silent until he has taken a good lead over his comrades. In the first the imperfection, although there, can easily be put up with because it does not harm the general work of the pack but in the second it should be considered a capital crime and cannot be tolerated.

The mute hound on the scent who hides it or keeps it secret not only does not try to help but makes every effort to outdistance all assistance and all company. Jealous of having the lead he follows this scent for a certain time without speaking as a result of which he forces his fellows to follow, straggling a long way behind.

Taking together the matters which we have discussed we conclude that the hound should neither be too free nor too shy of voice and that, when there is occasion for it, he should speak truthfully and thoughtfully.

PHYSICAL QUALITIES

The Nose. Fineness of nose or scenting capacity is the prime and inherited virtue which, inborn in the hound, becomes the source of its other merits. It can, perhaps, be placed amongst both the physical and the mental qualities, since if it belongs to the first by its origins, it sometimes enters into the realm of the other by its development.

The hound which begins with little scenting ability often finishes by acquiring it together with knowledge and skill and when he is older acknowledges the scent almost as well as individuals with better noses. He improves in nose inversely to the gun-dog which loses his as he ages. Is it, in the case of the hound, experience which allows him to recognise a scent or is it really the faculty of scenting which modifies and increases itself? We cannot say. But what is true is that a hound, cold of nose when it starts hunting, often corrects itself from this physical imperfection as it advances in age and wisdom.

These observations do not lessen the great advantage and incontestable superiority of hounds born with a really fine nose. Scenting better, they act with far more certainty and ease: their work is much more complete, more rapid and regular.

Hounds with fine noses are perfect *rapprocheurs**: They

* Note: The *rapprocheur* ("the bringer together") excels in the morning quest and in working up to the hare then or when, in the course of the hunt, she has squatted.

can quest on a trail long after sunrise and pick out a scent where others do not even stop. The sensibility of their nose prevents them from going back on the line or over-running it and lessens the dangers resulting from bad scenting conditions. They often hunt with head high, not lowering their noses, and their work is then more brilliant, more active and direct.

The Voice. A fine voice is among the requirements for a hound, not only for the pleasure which it gives but because of its value in hunting.

We know of Masters of Hounds who have no use for an individual with a poor voice. We would not be so exclusive and we do not suggest that excellent young hounds should be rejected only because their cry is poor but we insist most strongly that the hound with a good voice has a superiority and an undoubted value. He makes himself heard better when the line is hit off after a check and informs and rallies his fellows more promptly and surely. These advantages have a considerable bearing when one hunts in woodland or in country subject to fog and winds. The more resounding the voice, the better it directs hounds and huntsman who, in bad weather, can mistake their direction. The fine crier or *hurleur** also gives infinite pleasure; his vibrant and prolonged notes, dominating the clamorous orchestra of the pack, charm the ear of the Master, so attentive to this harmonious concert.

The voice, however, should be proportionate to the size and conformation of the hound. If it is too heavy in a little body it tires the organs and often saps the stamina and energy.

---

* Note: A *hurleur* ("howler") produces long-drawn notes as distinct from a series of "chopped" notes.

Hounds casting

The Comte Élie de Vezins with his hounds

Porcelaine hounds

Griffon bassets

The most esteemed voices are those which finish on the note "A", those like a bugle and those which are deep and prolonged. Hollow and heavy voices are perfect to accompany and garnish these but they should not be too numerous because their tone is not very sonorous or varied. Admirers of French hounds attach the greatest value to a fine voice. We entirely share their predilection and their demand because this merit, which also evidences purity of race, brings to the work of the pack one of its greatest attractions.

Stamina. Every animal required to carry out hard work should be able to stand up to it without weakening. This truth bears all its real significance when applied to the hound, whose onerous *rôle* demands an energetic temperament. The hound without stamina, however adequate in other respects, has no serious place in the pack. Worn out by long or fast hunts he has not the strength to make use of his talents. Following with difficulty his stronger comrades he struggles along without speaking, needing all his efforts to keep in touch with the pack and having neither the time nor the opportunity to perform any work whatever.

One does not like to include him when hunting jointly with a strange pack because one is doubtful of the result of a long hunt and fears to see him give up in public. He can be useful in the morning quest or when finding; he can account for some hares when hunting is carried out in conjunction with the gun, but on a long and hard hunt he saddens the Master who suffers as he watches his painful efforts.

The hound endowed with stamina maintains the same speed of work and pace whatever the length of the chase and possesses this quality, called *tenue,* so indispensible when hunting with hounds.

Speed. The *pied*, as we said at the beginning of this work, should be neither slow nor excessive : we repeat this.

A slow progression gives rise to a number of inconveniences which we have indicated in dealing with the hound which is too *collé*. If the reason is not the same it produces the same results and so as not to fatigue our readers we ask them to read again the section on the active hound.

Slow and languid hunts, in addition to the chances of failure which they present, finish by cooling the enthusiasm of those who follow them. Their spiritlessness, with the constant fear of a check, discourages everybody and threatens to such an extent the delay of a check and the difficulty of getting forward that even the most experienced Master feels impelled to holloa the hounds on when he views the hare a long way in front of them.

Much as we love the slow work of the morning or of the quest for the hare we are not attracted by those slow hunts which terminate, more often than not, by the loss of the hare or by a kill so little expected that one gets no pleasure from this unexpected success.

In a neighbouring country we have seen a pack of bassets hunting which, for half a day, followed its hare faultlessly and with the most perfect regularity but, whilst admiring the excellence of this little pack, we followed it without experiencing that feeling of excitement which whips the blood when a lively and animated hunt permits the Huntsman, at the end of two hours, to sound the joyous "Kill".

If we criticise the slow *pied* we are far from being partisans of excessive speed and we remain resolutely opposed to all extremes. We admit that a very fast progression can charm the eye and offer a moving spectacle but what inconveniences it occasions!

The hound which is carried away by too precipitate a style and in consequence is not able to be entirely certain and take note of ruses and twists is more likely to surpass and over-run the scent. By the rapidity of his work he accustoms himself to a hot scent which permits him on good days to keep near the quarry but he becomes less persistent and less active when unfavourable conditions oblige him to proceed more slowly and to work on a cold line. The advantages and charms of his voice are lost through his inability to produce it in the middle of his efforts whilst travelling so fast and one hears only short cries, so disagreeable to the ears of the French hunting man.

We appreciate that to hunt the larger animals, which defend themselves above all by their speed and stamina, one requires a hound of considerable speed because it is one of the requirements for success and avoids the necessity for *relais**, not generally in use at the present time. But to account for the hare, which offers real resistance only through its ruses and cleverness, we deplore too much speed and will have no part of this tendency which tries to relate two entirely different methods of hunting.

We would say to those who like these rapid chases, ending in a *hallali courant***, and in which the pleasures of the horse play as large a part as those of the hunt:

Create a pack for hunting the fox, that vermin which, in the course of the run will offer you a perpetual 'forrard on' and will enable you to enjoy the activity of your hounds and your horses. But leave to us the hunting of the hare; we who love it with its old traditions, its problems which,

---

* Notes: The *relais* formed part of the French system of stag-hunting. Several couples of hounds were kept back or placed in an advantageous position at the start of the hunt to be thrown in at head when the other hounds tired.

** The *hallali* is the kill and a *hallali courant* is therefore a kill "on the run", i.e. the quarry is overwhelmed and run into without difficulty.

although we do not seek to increase them, we accept in their entirety, convinced that our hounds will be able to unravel them even without the help of the zealous huntsman who, alas, often wishes, and always too soon, to substitute his own science for that of his hounds. Leave this to us who follow the vicissitudes of this skilful struggle on our carriage horses or sometimes on foot and who not only do not desire to shorten a spectacle from which we expect two hours of pleasure but which we should be desolated to see terminated in 40 or 45 minutes.

"The kill is the important thing, what do the means matter", some say to us, "so long as one achieves this result?". We do not share this reasoning. Hunts more or less difficult, more or less brilliant, leave a huntsman with very different impressions and very different satisfactions.

We come back, then, to the opinion which we have already expressed and which indicates for the *pied* a middle pace, vigorous and sustained, which permits the taking, in two hours, of a large hare.

Beauty and Distinction of Conformation. Beauty and distinction of conformation are the final and finishing touch to a good pack hound.

If these qualities have nothing to do with the merit of being a good hunting hound they have their importance by the satisfaction which they give. The possession of anything gives greater pleasure the more nearly the object approaches perfection of appearance. So the hound which unites to the merit of excellence in its work the fullest beauty and elegance is that which most flatters the pride of the Master and which consequently gives him the most pleasure.

We fully understand that as far as the hound is concerned excellence in its work is of the first importance and that one should not be carried away by beauty to the detriment of the working qualities but we consider also that the pack hound which has the honour to be destined to hunt should approach perfection as closely as possible so as to be in every way worthy of its privileged existence.

If the voice is the delight of the ear, beauty of conformation is that of the eye and the vision. Furthermore, the hound which is badly constructed cannot stand up to hard work and, sooner or later. weakens, either as regards its stamina, or in its speed or health.

Let us quote from the work of M. de la Conterie—his portrait of the perfect hound; our task will be easier, clearer and better said :

It is most important that whoever is forming a pack of hounds should select hounds of a suitable size and well-chosen for otherwise one will extract from them only a very imperfect pleasure. The height should be considered relative to that of the quarry which one tends to hunt but so far as signs of goodness and beauty are concerned, both of these qualities should be found in the small hound as well as in the large.

The hound, to be well-made and beautiful, should have the head well-made and longer than it is broad; the forehead wide; the eye large and bright; the nostrils well-opened and moist rather than dry; the ear low, narrow, hanging down and curled inwards and longer than the nose by only two inches. The body of a size and length proportionate to the limbs so that without being too long it may be more slender than stocky; the shoulders neither too wide nor too narrow; the back broad, high and arched; the haunches high and wide; the stern broad near the back but terminating like that of a rat and loosely curved in a half-circle; the thighs well tucked up and well muscled; the leg vigorous, the foot lean and the nails thick and short.

The height of hounds for the hare and the roe is from 21 to 23 inches; that of hounds for the stag from 25 to 28 inches; and that of hounds for the boar and wolf from 23 to 25 inches.

Equality of size and colour should be aimed at in a well-ordered pack. The brilliant picture of hunting on the quest and in the ensuing run together with beauty of colouring are benefits which are comprised in the exterior qualities and we do no more than draw attention to them.

The clear-cut colours are those which should be sought after because they are always esteemed in spite of the variations of fashion. Formerly orange-pied hounds were popular, then the black and white marked with tan on the head, and now very ticked or mottled hounds are preferred. One cannot discuss tastes; it is an axiom too well-known for us to presume to advise. In our opinion the colour of a hound is not of great importance; that it may, in the first place, work well and then be beautiful and of good conformation these are the principal factors which it is important and not always easy to unite.

Conclusion

We beg our readers to pardon us for the mass of detail comprised in our study of the hound but it seemed to us that one could not indicate too fully, so far as serious hare-hunting is concerned, how necessary it is to understand hounds well and to be able to judge with certainty and appreciate exactly their respective types, qualities and methods of use.

This deep knowledge is so much more necessary for the Master of Hounds, who must know how to create and organise his pack, that is to say, choose, classify and adjust his hounds so as to form a team which, by its wise selection, will combine all the talents and all the different styles of working. Again he must know how to make use in his country of the hounds which will suit it best and not be led away by preferences which will be harmful to his success.

To obtain good and practical results it is not necessary to be exclusive and unhappily this is the main fault of all hunting men, past, present and, I was going to say, future, forgetting that the future does not belong to man.

Huntsmen who like enterprising hounds refuse to recognise the merits of hounds which are calm, *collé* and *requérant* on the scent. The partisans of steady *chiens de centre* see no good in determined and ambitious hounds of a dangerous eagerness. Lovers of the *chiens d'ordre* have a profound contempt for the ordinary and poor-voiced *briquets.* The owners of *briquets* are crushing in their irony and sarcasm at the expense of the *grands chiens* which they consider only as show hounds, having no value outside the kennel and as models for hunting pictures. In a word each has a fixed, inflexible opinion and will not admit that any good can be found in what he does not like or does not possess. This is a temptation which every intelligent hunting man should avoid, always guarding himself against exclusive appreciations, for there is always a good and bad side which he must look for. Let us not, then, take sides but recognise good qualities wherever they are to be found and in whatever form they may present themselves, knowing how to apply our impartiality in the face of the true and the correct.

On this philosophical thought, dear readers, we will regretfully say good-bye, praying that St. Hubert will keep you in his holy care and that he will permit you to appreciate for many years the error or truth of our reflections.